Woode

What I Wish I'd Known When I Started

Jim Hamm

Acknowledgements

Reed Hamm inspired this book with a thoughtful suggestion. Lee and Reed Hamm both offered editorial and engineering insight.

Donna Hamm rendered her usual grammatical and spelling expertise. And, more importantly, steadfast encouragement for the past forty-three years.

Mary Hamm and Jonathan Williams gave most helpful editorial feedback.

Tim Baker, as always, provided keen insight.

All photos by Donna Hamm.

Bois d'Arc Press Copyright 2018

ALL RIGHTS RESERVED. No part of this book may be reproduced or transmitted in any form by any means, electronic or mechanical, including photocopying and recording, or by any information storage and retrieval system, except as may be expressly permitted by the 1976 Copyright Act or in writing from the publisher. Requests for permission should be addressed to:

Bois d'Arc Press, PO Box 87, Goldthwaite, TX 76844.

ISBN 9781980958000

Dedication

To Tim Baker, for his unparalleled contributions to natural archery.
To Paul Comstock, the bugler in the whitewood bow revolution.
To the late Jay Massey, who originally stood alone against the tide.
Everyone who makes a wooden bow today works in their shadows.

Table of Contents

Acknowledgements 2
Dedication... 3
Table of Contents 4
Foreword 5
Important Terms 6
Tools Needed... 7
Selecting and Cutting Wood........................... 8
Rule 1: Follow Wood Fibers on the Back of the Bow ... 14
Rule 2: Design For the Specific Gravity of the Wood Species ... 16
Bowstring 23
Rule 3: Tiller Correctly 28
Finishing 42
Arrows 48
Shooting... 50
You've Made Several Successful Bows, Now What? 53
Afterword 55
Appendix... 57
Recommended Reading 60

Foreword

By making and shooting a wooden bow, you'll be joining a brotherhood of bowyers stretching back to your 500th grandfather. Think of it this way - if wooden bows weren't effective, you wouldn't be here. None of us would.

In practice, a wooden bow is a time machine. The patience and pride of craftsmanship remain the same today as they have been for the past fifteen thousand years. Once a bow is freed from its wooden prison by skill and intuition, it becomes almost a living being, an extension of the bowyer.

After spending more than four decades making well over a thousand wooden bows, I have pretty well perfected the process. I have also made about every conceivable mistake possible, as well as a few that are inconceivable. When I started decades ago, there were virtually no books to offer guidance, and no mentors to be found. I learned largely by the trial and error method, with emphasis on the error. All of that experience and mistakes are chronicled in the bowmaking books I've written. In particular, helping to write, edit, and publish *The Traditional Bowyer's Bible* series of four books was a high-water mark both personally and professionally. So I figured I had said my piece on the subject.

Recently, however, it was casually suggested by one of my sons that I put down some thoughts on what I wish I'd known way back when I started.

That suggestion sparked this book. Please note that "What I Wish I'd Known" is in bold text throughout the book.

Now, making bows from wood is a vast subject when considering they've been made for upwards of fifteen millennia by thousands of cultures all over the world. Short, long, flat, recurved, crowned, from hundreds of different woods, with sinew backs and horn bellies, for warfare, for use in forests and on horseback and in the Arctic, for hunting to feed families, and for recreation and competition. A vast subject, indeed, and covered in depth with over 500,000 words in *The Traditional Bowyer's Bibles*. But, if taking the first steps down the path of hand crafting weapons, you don't need to know all of that. Not yet. All that's required right now is the very essence of how to design and make a quality wooden bow.

Let's dive right in.

> **WHAT I WISH I'D KNOWN**
> **Three Bedrock Rules of Bowmaking:**
> 1. Follow wood fibers on the back of the bow.
> 2. Design the bow for the specific gravity (density) of the wood species.
> 3. Tiller correctly.
> Adhere to these three simple rules and you'll have a successful bow.

Important Terms

Back – The side of the bow away from the archer.

Belly – The side of the bow facing the archer.

Brace height – When strung, the distance from the belly of the bow to the string. Adjusted with string length.

Draw length – The distance (in inches) a given archer pulls an arrow to reach full draw.

Draw weight – The amount of force (in pounds) required to pull a bow to full draw.

Fadeouts or Fades – On a flatbow, the widest part of the bow, measured from one side to the other.

Full draw – When an arrow is pulled to the archer's maximum draw length, and the bow reaches its maximum draw weight.

Mass – The physical weight of the bow, measured in ounces. (I understand that mass does not equal physical weight, but we will use this definition for our bowmaking purposes).

Nock – Notches cut in the tips of the bow to hold the string. Also a notch at the back of the arrow to place on the string.

String follow or Set – The amount the limbs of a bow are permanently bent. Calculated by laying the unstrung bow back-down on a flat surface and measuring the distance from the surface to the tip.

Tiller, tillering – Removing wood from a bow's belly to make it bend evenly, while obtaining the desired draw weight.

Tools Needed

Basic Tools
- Hatchet
- Rasp
- Pocket knife for scraper
- Small rattail file or chainsaw file
- Tillering stick
- Sandpaper (220, 320, 400, 600 grit)

Fine bows can be made with the simplest of tools.

Useful Additional Tools
- Gooseneck scraper or cabinet scraper
- Cabinetmaker's fine rasp
- Sanding block
- Chainsaw
- Wedges
- Bandsaw

Some additional tools help speed up the process.

Selecting and Cutting Wood

I'm a big proponent of using woods available in a local area, and this is especially important for beginners. By utilizing local wood, the cost is low and the availability high, which means the bowyer can easily experiment and grow.

> **WHAT I WISH I'D KNOWN**
> Beginners should start with whitewoods; ash, birch, cherry, elm, hickory, hop hornbeam, maple, and oak, among others.

Look for hardwoods with over 0.50 specific gravity (or density), with water being the benchmark at 1.00.

For beginners, it's important to choose hardwoods known as "white woods", or woods that are all or mostly sapwood; primarily ash, birch, cherry, elm, hickory, hop hornbeam, maple, and oak, among others. A subspecies of some or most of these woods grow in the vast majority of North America.

With whitewoods such as hickory, left, the bow's back is the outside of the stave. Osage orange, right, showing dark heartwood and the lighter sapwood that must be removed.

The primary reason for using these woods, even beyond their availability, is the outer ring of wood directly under the bark will be the back of the bow.

The problem with other hardwoods, such as Osage orange (or bois d'arc), mulberry, black locust, and walnut, among others, is that they have a thin layer of sapwood over the dense inner heartwood, meaning that some or all of the sapwood should be removed to make a bow. A tedious, exacting process of removing wood down to a single yearly growth ring of heartwood for the bow's back. Making bows from these woods is a worthy endeavor, but not really for beginners.

With the whitewoods, however, remove the bark and there's the bow's finished back. Nothing could be easier or simpler.

After identifying the species in the area to use, cut whitewoods in the fall or winter after the outer growth ring is fully developed for the year. It's easier to evaluate a tree's qualities after the leaves have fallen, too. Select trees that are straight, at least 10 inches in diameter, 70-75 inches long, no twist apparent in the bark, and no knots or branches. A larger diameter tree reduces the crown on the back of the bow; longer allows more margin for bow layout. Bigger trees naturally yield more bowstaves, too. Being selective may require several days of searching to find near perfect trees, but the time spent will be more than repaid once the bowmaking begins, as it's far easier to make a first bow if there are no problems or "character" to overcome.

> **WHAT I WISH I'D KNOWN**
> Be very selective when choosing which trees to harvest.

As soon as a tree hits the ground and the section of log cut free, seal both ends with paint or glue. This prevents moisture from evaporating, which can cause "end checks" or cracks, and damage several inches of wood on each end.

It is advantageous to split the wood into staves as soon as possible. Tap a hatchet into the edge of one end, start a crack, then drive wedges into the crack to split the log.

The splitting continues until each stave is about 2 inches wide across the outside. Immediately remove the bark to help prevent insect damage and speed drying. In most cases a drawknife or knife blade inserted under one end begins the process, and the bark can be worked free relatively intact. Don't worry if there is a thin layer of inner bark (a layer of cambium) left behind.

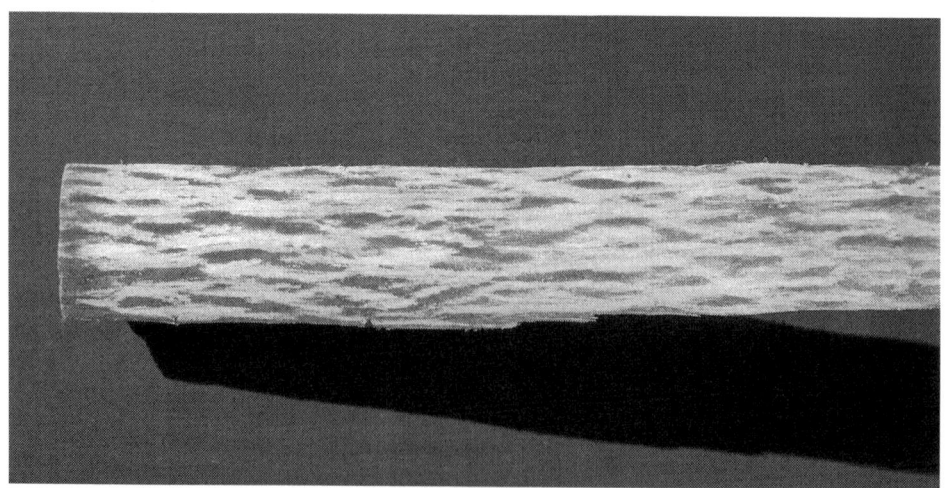

A thin layer of darker cambium sometimes remains after bark removal, which acts as camouflage for the finished bow.

One note about elm. It is an excellent bow wood, but difficult to split due to interlocking grain; the staves usually have to be chopped apart between the wedges.

It's important to understand the difference between growth rings and wood grain. The growth rings are concentric circles, while the grain is at right angles from the center of the log to the outside. Think of it as if a growth ring is the tire of a bicycle wheel, while the grain is the spokes. Logs and staves split along the grain. See photos on the next page.

Once the staves are split and the bark removed, store them indoors, preferably, but in any case protected from moisture. Storing staves indoors helps protect them from possible damage by wood-boring insects in warm weather. I've also seen cases where freshly cut wood was stored in an unheated shed, and below zero temperatures froze the high moisture content in the staves, irretrievably cracking them just like ice cracks a water pipe and rendering them worthless for bowmaking.

The relation of grain to yearly growth rings.

Grain radiates from the center of the log to the outside; wood splits and cracks along the grain.

Orientation of growth rings. A) Conventional stave. B) Flat-ringed lumber. C) Bias-ringed lumber. D) Edge-ringed lumber.

Can't find suitable wood or want to start making a bow today? Use lumber from the whitewood species listed above as well as those in the appendix. Lumber can be used to make natural bows since, after all, wood is wood. But there's a very important, though simple, caveat. The growth ring lines on the flat side of the board, the bow's future back, are the edges of yearly growth rings, and must, MUST, be perfectly straight from one end of the board to the other. No wiggles, islands, angling off the side of the board, meandering, or areas where the growth rings come to a point. None, zero, nada!

If the lines of the growth rings are straight, then the board can be crafted into a bow. Finding a suitable board often requires just as much dedication as finding a straight tree; perhaps one in a hundred qualifies.

> **WHAT I WISH I'D KNOWN**
> Regarding lumber for bows: the growth ring lines on the flat side of the board, the bow's future back, are the edges of yearly growth rings, and must, MUST, be perfectly straight from one end of the board to the other.

Suitable board, full length and closeup. The growth ring lines run straight and parallel from one end to the other. No wiggles, islands, angling off the side of the board, meandering, or growth rings coming to a point.

Unsuitable board, full length and closeup. A bow made from this board would break the first time it was pulled.

Rule 1: Follow Wood Fibers on the Back of the Bow

After the bark is removed from a whitewood stave, the wood fibers of the outer growth ring are perfectly intact, fulfilling the first rule of bowmaking. With Osage orange, removing wood down to an interior growth ring to faithfully follow the wood fibers means chasing the dips and dives and knots wherever they lead, a job the whitewood staves conveniently perform on their own.

> **WHAT I WISH I'D KNOWN**
> Using whitewoods along with careful layout ensures the wood fibers are intact on the back of the bow.

Wood fibers don't care which way they are bent, the wind might blow out of the east one day, the south the next, and then the north. As long as the wood fibers remain intact on the back of the bow, the bow is sound. And that's the reason bows can be made of either flat, biased, or edge-ringed lumber, as long as the growth ring lines on the board are straight, as outlined earlier, the wood fibers are intact. If the fibers are violated, either by cutting through growth rings or not following the grain, a weak point develops between the unjoined fibers, and they separate, which leads to a broken bow, bruised egos, and another trip to the lumber yard or wood lot.

Once the back of the bow is established on a stave, the longitudinal grain must be followed as well for the fibers to remain intact the full length of the bow. While holding one eye near the end of the stave, and positioning the stave between your eye and a light source, the longitudinal grain can be easier to see, appearing as small scratches in the wood surface. Use a pencil to lightly draw a line from the middle of one end of the stave to the middle of the other, carefully following the grain throughout. Follow slight meanders, especially around knots, if any. The centerline will closely parallel the split sides. If the stave is straight and clean, the line will be virtually straight.

This pencil line will be the centerline of the bow as it is laid out.

Draw a line the length of stave following the grain.

Rule 2: Design For the Specific Gravity of the Wood Species

From a practical standpoint with regard to bowmaking, "wood is wood". The primary quality that must be known of a given wood species is its specific gravity, or density. Lighter weight woods should be made comparatively wider and/or longer than denser, heavier wood. This wider design for lighter woods yields more surface area to handle the strain of tension and compression.

There is little "magic" in any particular species, hundreds of species have been successfully used since the ancient advent of archery.

Don't believe me? The proof that "wood is wood" is that properly designed bows of the same length of vastly different woods will all have about the same mass, or physical weight. This it true even though the lighter wood will have wider, thinner, limbs than the heavier wood. There will be the same amount of "wood" in each bow, and therefore the two bows will perform the same. Another way to look at it is the only practical difference between hickory and ash is that the ash has more air in it, so more total volume of material is necessary to achieve the same mass of wood.

> **WHAT I WISH I'D KNOWN**
> **The primary wood characteristic a bowyer must know to properly design a bow is the specific gravity (density) of the wood species.**

For a given weight bow the bowyer just needs the specific gravity (density) of the chosen wood in order to match the bow design to the species. Please read the preceding sentence again, as this is one of the most important aspects of bowmaking I wish I had known when I first began.

After determining draw length (see photo), the design of the bow can begin. There are a couple of design options here.

Measure draw length to the front of the bow hand

> **WHAT I WISH I'D KNOWN**
> **Different wood species impact bow design, but not bow performance.**

One is the classic D bow (so-called because of the side view shape when strung), with the widest part of the bow at the handle. I think of this style of bow as the grandfather of all bows since it is the simplest to make and tiller.

The other design is the flatbow, or one with a narrowed grip section flaring out to wider, thinner limbs, which then taper to the tips.

Assuming the same species of wood and the same draw weight and draw length, a D bow must be made longer than a flatbow. Keep in mind that, given the same wood species, both types of bows should have about the same surface area of working limb and the same mass. So, since the D bow is narrower, it must be longer.

D Bow

The following designs are for a 28-inch draw length and a 45-pound draw weight. If using a longer or shorter draw length, bow design lengths can be adjusted proportionally.

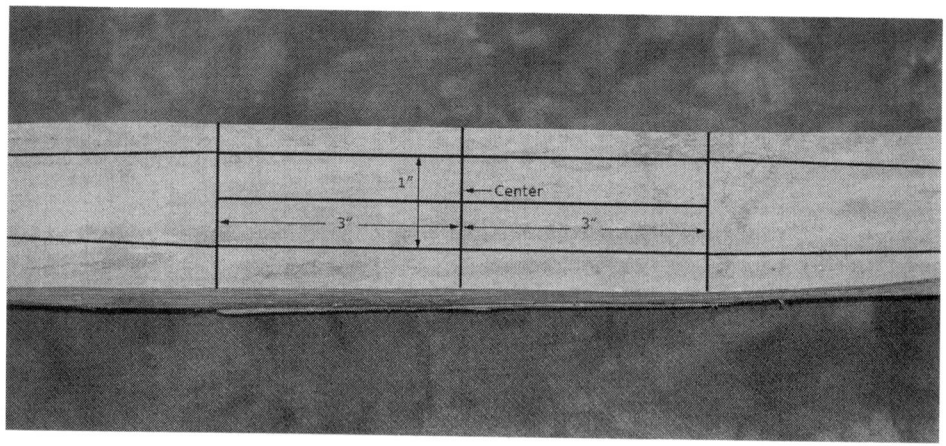

Longbow (D bow) handle dimensions.

All D bows begin with the same thickness dimensions and are used along with the width dimensions shown in the D Bow photo:
Handle – 1 ¼" thick
Tips – ½" thick

For a hickory or oak D bow, specific gravity (S/G) 0.68, the back profile should be as follows:
Length – 70"
Width at handle – 1" for 3" either side of bow's center for a total of 6"
Width at tips – 1/2".
Woods with a specific gravity less than hickory's 0.68 should be made longer; those with a specific gravity heavier than hickory shorter. Some examples:
Cherry, cedar elm or winged elm, hop hornbeam, S/G 0.65:
Length – increase to 71" with same width profile.

Ash, birch, denser maples, S/G 0.60:
Length – increase to 74", with same width profile.

Hackberry, lighter elms, lighter maples, S/G 0.50:
Length – increase to 76", with same width profile.
These lengths should be longer if a draw weight heavier than 45 pounds is desired, or for a lighter draw weight, they can be shorter.

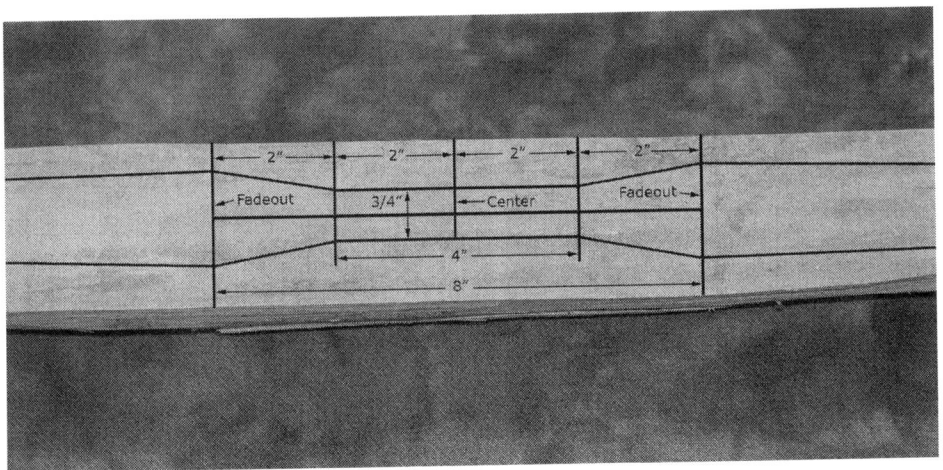

Flatbow handle with fadeout dimensions.

Flatbow

The following designs are for a 28-inch draw length and a 45-pound draw weight. If using a longer or shorter draw length, bow design lengths can be adjusted proportionally.

Note that handle measurements are the same for all wood species. Measure half the total length to find the center of the bow, then in each direction from center measure 2 inches for a grip section (total of 4 inches), then another 2 inches to fadeout. The total from one fadeout to the other is 8 inches. All handle sections are ¾ inch wide for the center 4 inches of grip, flaring to the fadeouts, the widest part of the bow:

Hickory or oak, S/G 0.68:
Length – 67"
4" handle section -1 ¼" thick, then taper to fadeouts
Width at fadeouts – 1 ½"
Thickness at fadeouts – ¾"
Width at tips – ½"
Thickness at tips – ½"

Cherry, cedar elm or winged elm, hop hornbeam, S/G 0.65:
Length – 67"
4" handle section -1 ¼" thick, then taper to fadeouts
Width at fadeouts – 1 5/8"
Thickness at fadeouts – ¾"
Width at tips – ½"

Thickness at tips – ½"

Ash, birch, denser maples, S/G 0.60:
Length – 67"
4" handle section -1 ¼" thick, then taper to fadeouts
Width at fadeouts – 1 ¾"
Thickness at fadeouts – ¾"
Width at tips – ½"
Thickness at tips – ½"

Hackberry, lighter elms, lighter maples, S/G 0.50:
Length – 67"
4" handle section -1 ¼" thick, then taper to fadeouts
Width at fadeouts – 2"
Thickness at fadeouts – ¾"
Width at tips – ½"
Thickness at tips – ½"

Once again, in the D bow and flatbow dimensions given above, the design is tailored to the specific gravity of the wood species as well as the desired draw weight and draw length. Note that the thickness dimensions given are the same, but are merely starting points. The final thickness will resolve itself during the tillering process, as thickness can only be determined by the characteristics of each individual bow stave and the desired finished weight.

> **WHAT I WISH I'D KNOWN**
> **When considering design, a longer bow is under less strain and is easier to shoot accurately.**

The old benchmark was to make a bow at least the height of the archer, and as a general rule it's a good idea to err on the side of extra length. A longer bow is under less strain and is easier to shoot accurately.

After some experience, a hybrid of the two designs can be made, where the handle only slightly flares out to the fadeouts, then tapers to the tips.

Also after some experience, it's advantageous to make the tips as narrow as possible. This reduces mass where it has the most negative effect; the tips move the furthest during the shot. Lighter tips produce slightly faster arrow flight as well as reduced hand shock felt in the bow arm when the arrow is released.

In any case, after deciding upon a design, start with the centerline drawn down the length of the stave. Then lay out the chosen design with one-half of the dimensions on either side of the centerline.

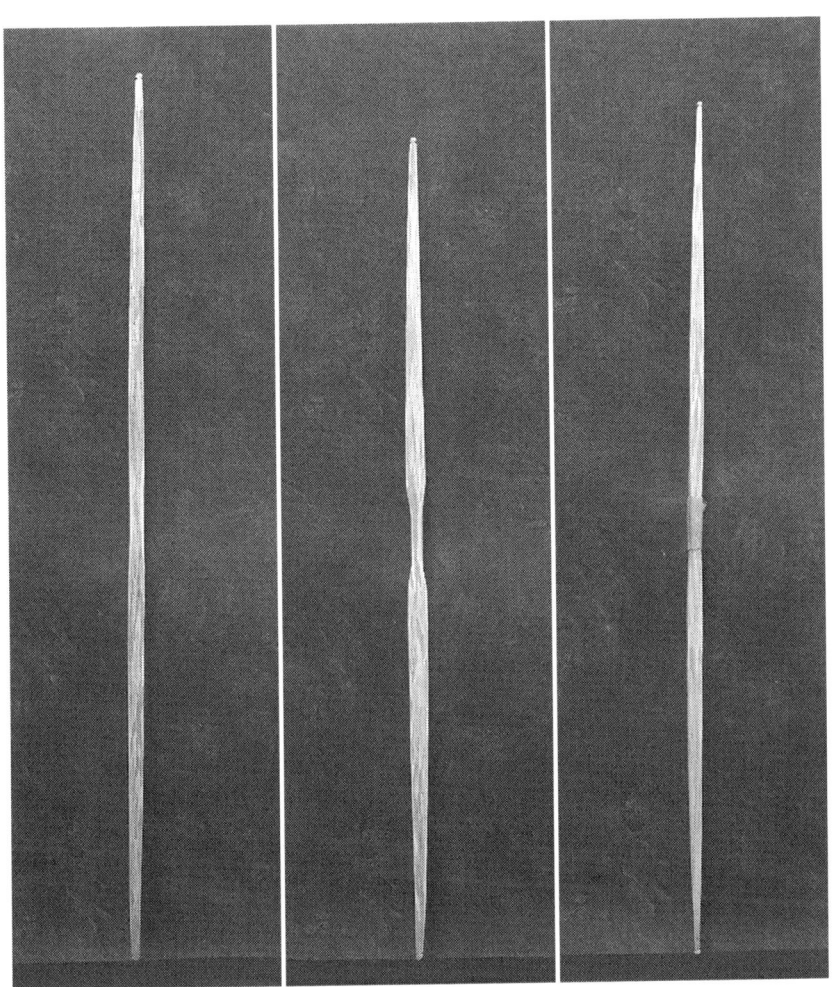

Longbow profile, left. Flatbow profile, center. Hybrid profile, right, long design with slightly wider limbs and narrowed handle.

Reduce the stave close to the profile lines with a bandsaw, or very carefully with a hatchet. When chopping with a hatchet, always work from the center of the stave toward the tip for a D bow, or from the fadeout toward the tip with a flatbow. Remove the remaining wood with a rasp until the chosen profile is complete.

At this point, the second rule of bowmaking: Design for the Specific Gravity of the Wood Species, has been fulfilled. All that remains is the final step: Tiller Correctly.

But first, it's time to make a string.

Bowstring

A string made from natural fibers is a thing of beauty in its own right. It also has a lineage even older than wooden bows. Making cordage, along with firemaking, are two of the oldest human skills. A string of flax, hemp, sinew, or gut just looks right on a handmade wooden bow. Crafting a bow-worthy string of natural fibers is certainly a worthy goal, though far from easy. In fact, it may well be a skill equal in time and expertise to bowmaking.

So, for now, if this is your first foray into natural archery, concentrate on the bowmaking portion by purchasing a spool of Dacron B-50. Just keep the allure of natural fiber strings in the back of your mind until you master Stringmaking 101.

> **WHAT I WISH I'D KNOWN**
> Make the string long. It's used as a tillering string first, then shortened to use for the bowstring.

The Dacron string is used as a tillering string first, then shortened to use for the bowstring. Make the string from two seven-strand halves reverse-wrapped around each other. There are other string configurations, for example with more bundles and less threads per bundle, but for now stick with the basic seven-strand, two bundle string.

First, pull out a single strand a full two arm-spans long from the spool, then add another two feet or so and cut it free. It's better to make it too long than not quite long enough. Do this six more times until there are a total of seven threads. Stagger the ends over a couple of inches, then smooth the bundle of threads together lengthways. B-50 is lightly waxed, so the threads will stick together. Make sure there are no wiggles, loops, or slack places in any of the individual threads in the bundle. Place this bundle aside.

Make another identical bundle of seven threads. With a thumb and forefinger, hold both bundles about 4 inches from the staggered end (see photo). Each individual bundle will be twisted clockwise, while the bundles are wrapped around each other counterclockwise.

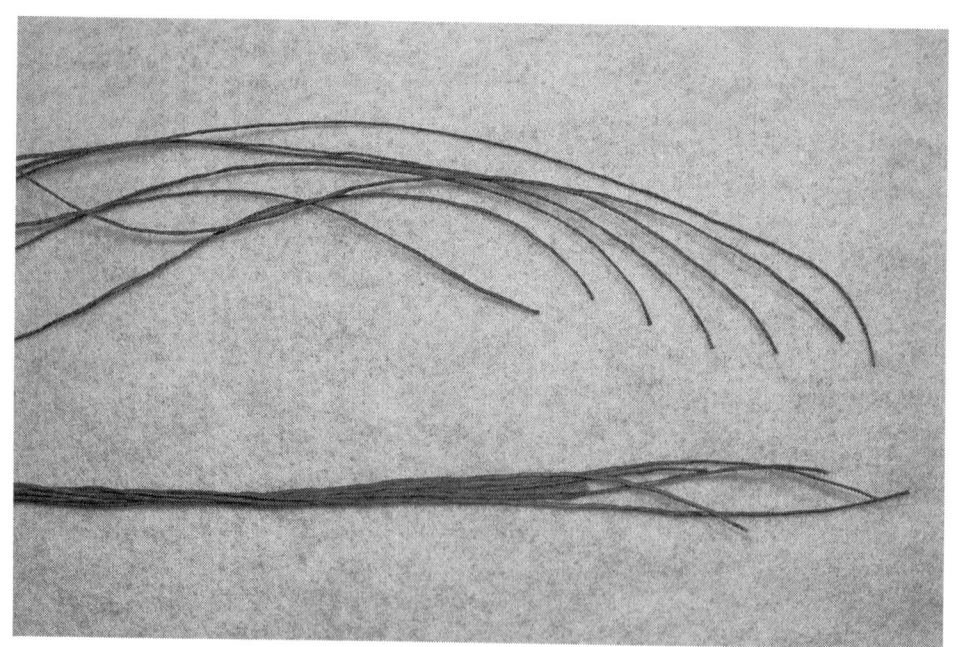

Staggering the ends of the threads.

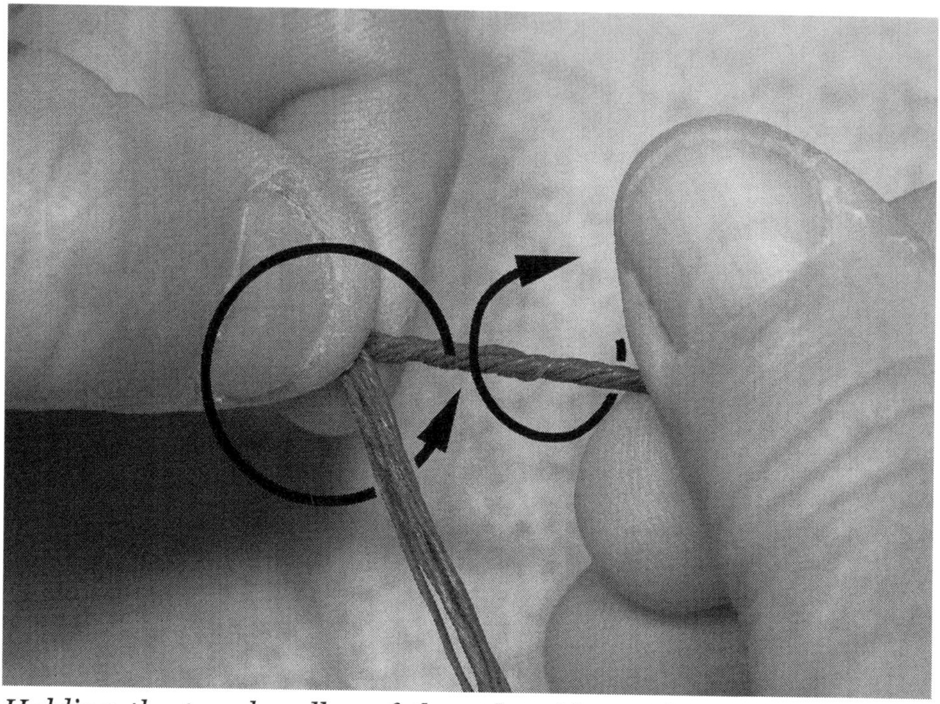

Holding the two bundles of threads with one hand and twisting with the other.

Start with the furthest bundle, and twist it clockwise with the right hand, then lay it over the other bundle counterclockwise. Move the thumb and forefinger of the left hand up slightly to hold this twist in the bundles. Again, twist the furthest (second) bundle clockwise, then lay it over the first bundle counterclockwise. Move the fingers of the left hand forward slightly to hold the latest twist.

Continue until about 2 inches are reverse-twisted together; this will become the loop for the bowstring. It has to be long enough to fit comfortably over one bow limb, but not so large that it will be sloppy and fall all the way down the limb to the handle. The size of the loop will vary, depending on bow design, and forming the perfectly sized loop will be one of the more frustrating parts of beginner string-making.

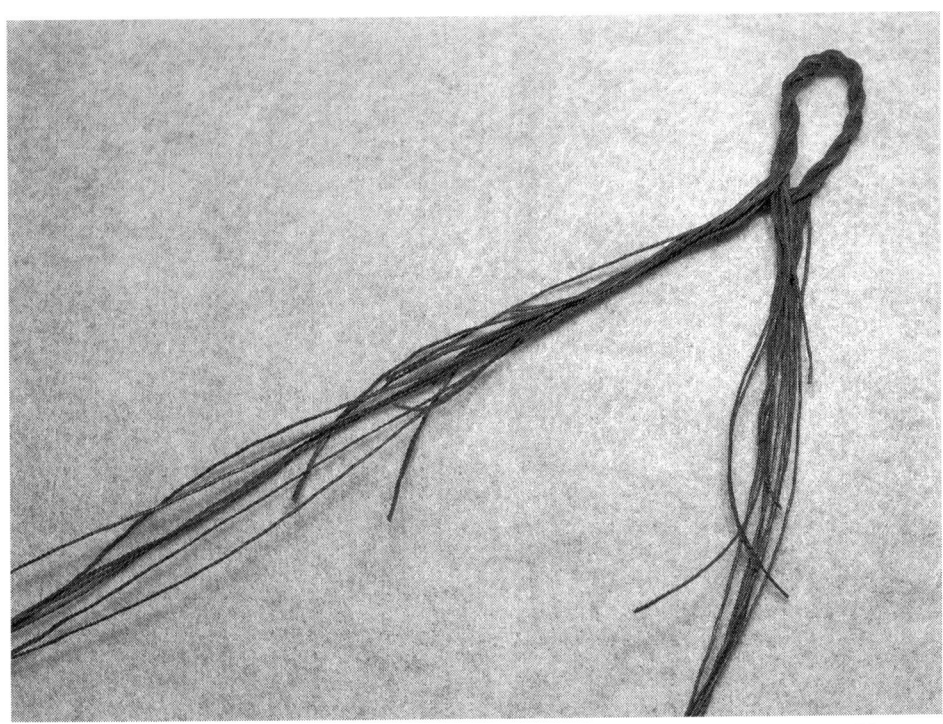

Loop laid into string. Note how tapered ends of each bundle are blended back into the main bundles.

Fold the twisted portion over to form the loop. Place the short tapered tail of one bundle together with one long main bundle, and the other short tapered tail together with the other main bundle (see photo). Use the fingers of the left hand to hold this intersection in

Reverse twisting continued and loop completed. Note that tapered ends allow a smooth transition back to basic string. Snip off ends of protruding single threads.

Timber Hitch. A secure knot for the bottom limb that allows easy length adjustment.

place, then simply continue with the reverse twisting of the bundles as before.

As the string progresses, it will become clear why the ends were staggered, so there will be a smooth taper as they are absorbed into the main string, rather than a sharp dropoff where all the strands terminate at once.

Continue reverse twisting for the entire length of the bundles. When the individual threads start to run out at the end, place an overhand knot in the entire string to hold the twists in place. Cut off any tail ends past this knot.

Refer to the photo for tying the timber hitch: a slip knot that will not come loose when tied, but is easy to manipulate to adjust the length of the string. By using the timber hitch for one end rather than a loop in both ends, the string can be used for both a long tillering string and later for a shorter bowstring as well.

Rule 3: Tiller Correctly

Tillering is where bowmaking really begins, when a stave that resembles a fencepost or a length of lumber that looks more like a walking stick starts to bend. By bending, it starts storing energy, a wonderful transformation as a bow emerges from its wooden prison.

> **WHAT I WISH I'D KNOWN**
> **The thickness taper on the sides of the bow must always be even, with no thick or thin areas. If the thickness tapers are correct, then the bow will bend evenly.**

The essence of tillering, a bedrock fact to keep firmly in mind, is that the thickness taper on the sides of the bow MUST always be even, with no thick or thin sections. This is one of the things I wish I had understood when I first started.

If the thickness taper is correct, then the bow will bend evenly, with no areas bending too much or not bending enough. Every portion of the bow does its fair share of the work, which makes it much more durable and efficient.

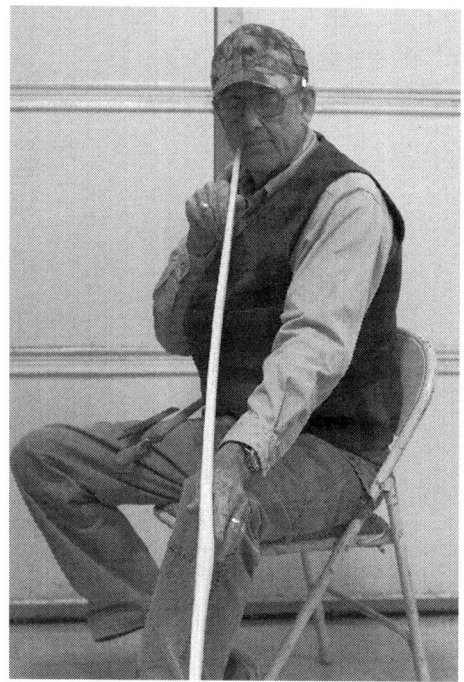

Smooth thickness taper is essential to successful tillering. Viewing from a flat angle near the tip makes it easier to see.

All of the thickness measurements given in the layout section earlier are starting points only; they are well above finished dimensions. The reasons for this are simple. First, a beginning bowyer feels blindly for the edge of the cliff, and the extra thickness is a safety margin. And second, the final thickness can be tailored only by the individual piece of wood and the individual design.

Begin by floor tillering, which is placing one bow tip on the ground (padded with a scrap of carpet or on your boot) and leaning into the stave while sighting down it. Do this with both limbs. This will give an idea of the weight of the draw. No doubt at this stage it will be far too stiff, requiring wood removal.

Use a rasp to reduce thickness evenly. For a D bow, remove wood from the center of the bow to the tips. For a flatbow, take off wood only from the fadeouts to the tips. When removing wood, make certain that the thickness taper remains even from the thickest portion to the thinnest.

> **WHAT I WISH I'D KNOWN**
> **Freshly cut whitewood can be taken all the way through the floor tillering stage, then quick-dried for 30 days and completed.**

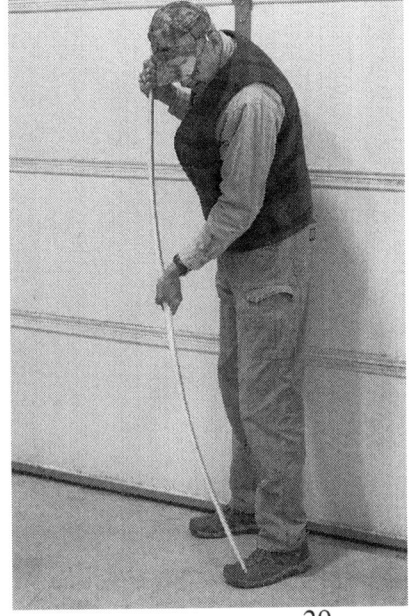

Floor tillering

Continue leaning into the bow and removing wood until the limbs start to bend. If using freshly cut whitewood, the stave can be taken all the way through this step, then stored flat for 30 days with good airflow. This will reduce moisture content to the level of "seasoned" wood much more quickly, then continue tillering.

Once bow limbs bend about the same amount, cut nocks in the tips for the bowstring with a chainsaw file or rattail file. If making a flatbow, now is the time to narrow the handle section down to the profile pencil lines drawn earlier.

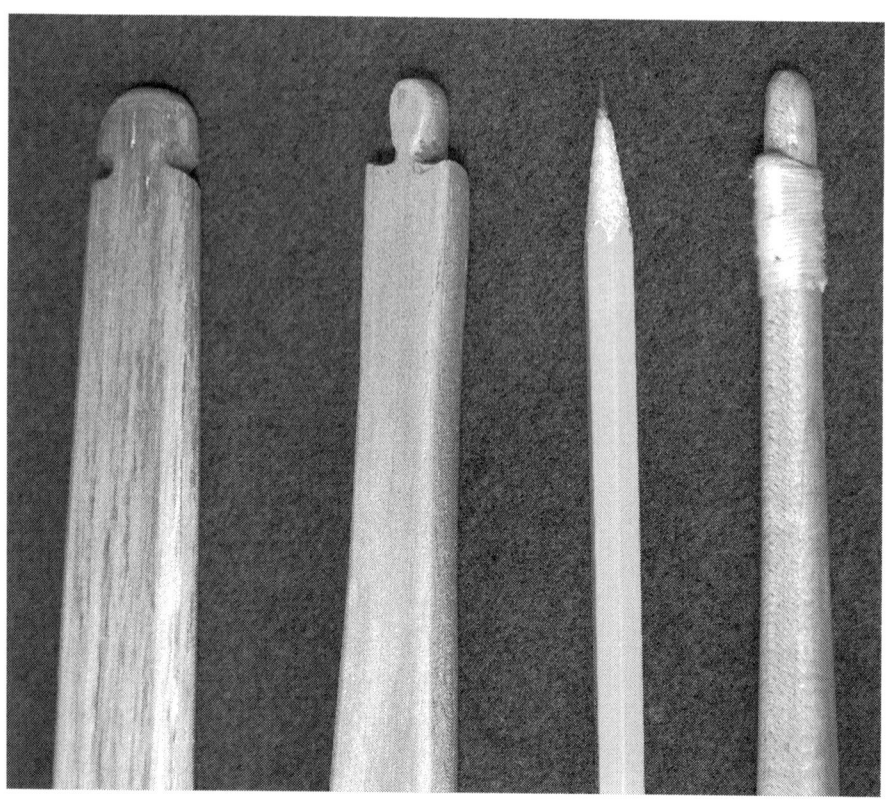

Left to right. Conventional nock, pin nock, a pencil for comparison, and a very narrow tip with wrap-on nock. The first two are standard nocks, found on the majority of wooden bows. The latter nock should be attempted only after successful completion of several bows.

This is a good opportunity to talk about finished bow drawweight. In my opinion, a first bow should be easy to shoot, not over

50 pounds, with 40-45 pounds even better. It's impossible to shoot well if the archer struggles to reach full draw.

> **WHAT I WISH I'D KNOWN**
> A bow should be easy to shoot fifty times without tiring. An archer will find accuracy elusive if unable to reach a consistent full draw.

Consider a heavy bow vs. a moderate bow. A 70-pound bow will shoot an arrow about 170 feet per second, a 50 pound bow about 150 fps. The 70-pound bow is 40% harder to pull but only 13% faster, not a very good tradeoff!

Archery is all about shot placement whether hunting or target shooting. A heavier weight bow is exactly like a larger caliber rifle, its use is not just irrelevant, but detrimental if it contributes to a miss.

Art Young, one of the namesakes of the Pope and Young Club, once said he could kill the biggest bear in Alaska with a 50-pound bow. We should defer to his judgement and make our bows no heavier than that, at least in the beginning.

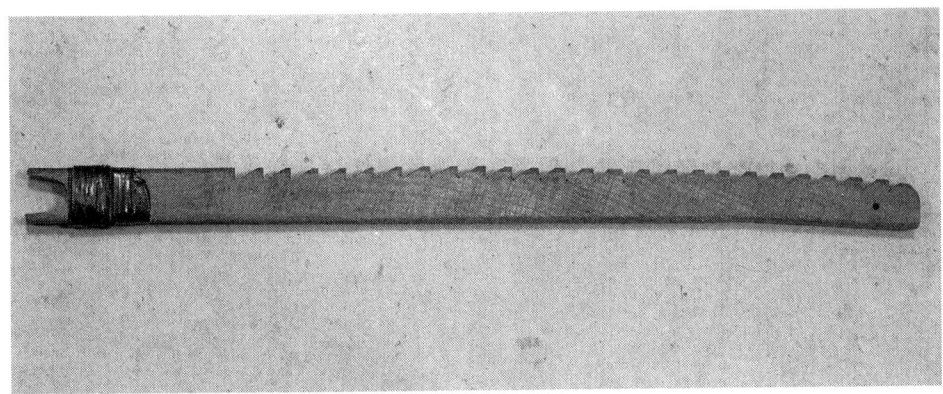

Tillering Stick

Place the bowstring loop in the nocks at one end of the bow, then secure the string in the other nock with a timber hitch. Put the center of the bow handle in the notch at the end of the tillering stick, then pull the string down to bend the limbs a bit and hook the center of the string in a side notch.

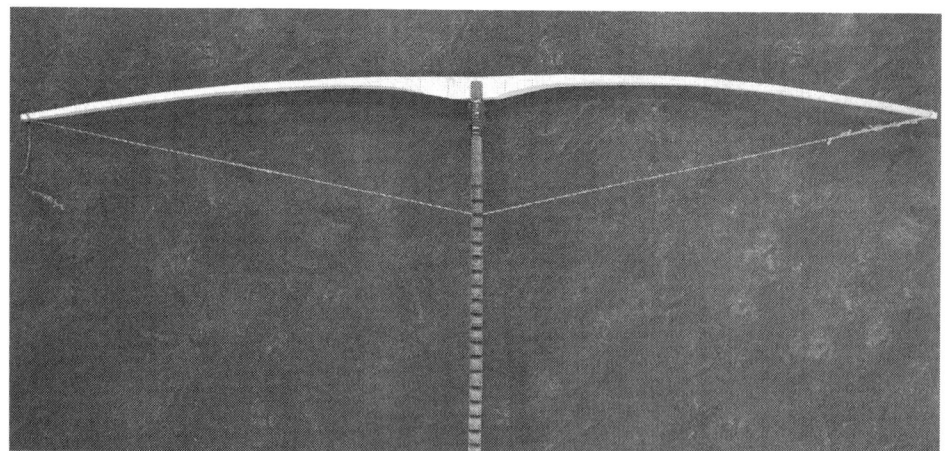

Pulling bow with long string on tillering stick. Left limb is slightly stiffer; wood should be removed only from this limb until both limbs bend evenly.

Note how the limbs are bending. If an area is stiff, or not bending enough, mark the belly lengthwise with a pencil. If any area bends too much, make an X on the belly with a pencil and do not remove wood in that area. If one limb is clearly stiffer than the other, mark that limb only for wood removal.

With a rasp, remove wood from the belly in the marked areas. Make long sweeping strokes with the rasp, moving longitudinally down the limb, rather than straight across the limb, which tends to dig a hole and make a thin spot.

When tillering, regularly look down the side of the limb with one eye right above the tip; any thick or thin areas will then be more apparent. Mark the limbs on the belly with a pencil and remove wood as needed. The thickness taper must remain even, and both sides of the limb must be the same thickness. The ideal is for the belly of the bow to be flat, as this gives the maximum area to resist compression, which minimizes string follow.

Replace the bow on the tillering stick and pull it again. Mark any areas that bend too much or not enough. Remove wood as before. The goal is to make both limbs bend evenly while bending the same amount.

The bow is now ready to string. Place the loop over one bow limb 3 inches from the tip. Retie the timber hitch on the other limb to take the slack out of the string. Step through the bow as shown, bend the bow, and slide the loop into the nocks in the

Step-through bow stringing. Be certain to keep the handle section on the hip.

upper tip. If the bow is too stiff to string, remove more wood as before until it can be strung.

The Dacron string may stretch and relax, which is normal, even to the point the bow is straight again. If so, shorten the string two inches. When the bow is strung, the string should stand away from the handle a couple of inches.

It will now become much more apparent how the limbs are bending. If one limb looks obviously stronger than the other, mark it and concentrate wood removal on that limb. Wood can be removed with the rasp while the bow is strung, but care must be taken not to damage the bowstring.

When both limbs are bending smoothly, and bending the same amount, replace the bow on the tillering stick and pull the string to only 1/3 draw (note that a bow should never be drawn past its final intended weight.) It is often helpful to prop the tillering stick and strung bow against a wall and take a few steps back. Flip the bow around and examine the other side, too. Observing the tiller from both sides is important as the natural contour of the wood, particularly

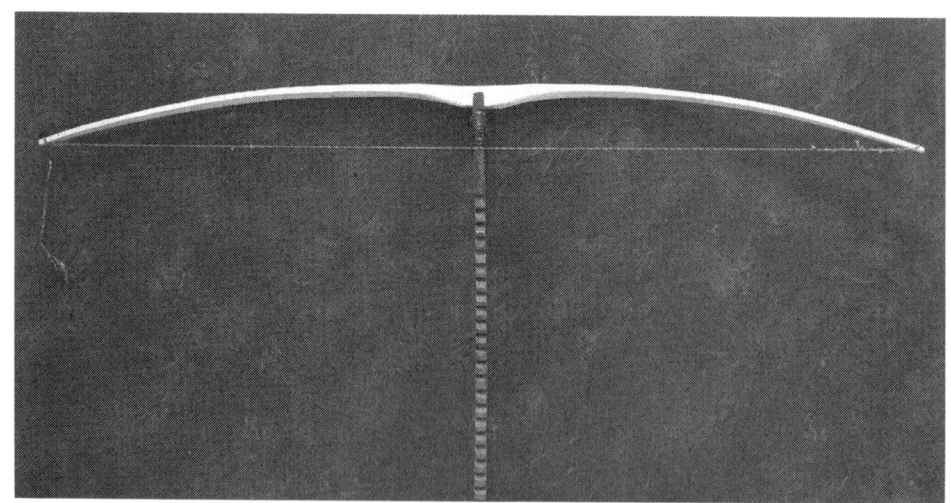

Flat bow first strung on tillering stick.

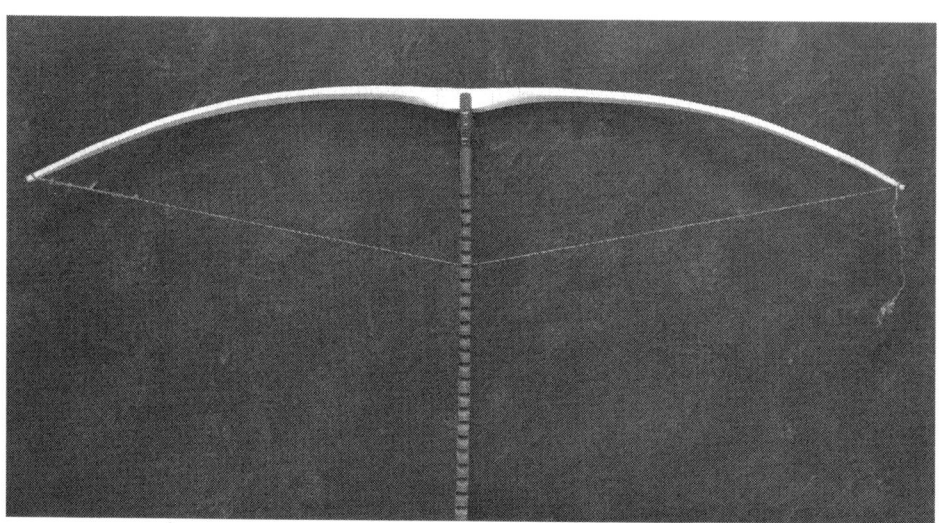

Flat bow first pulled to about one-third draw length. Right limb is a little stiffer and should have wood evenly removed for its entire length.

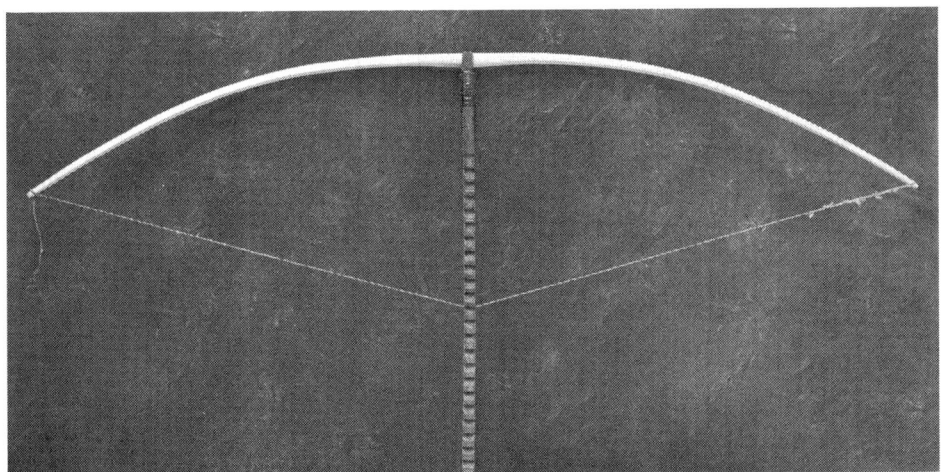

Longbow first drawn to about one-third draw length. Right limb is stiffer from about mid-limb to tip and should have wood evenly removed from this area.

from tree staves, can mask tillering errors. Mark any areas that bend too much or are too stiff and remove wood as before.

Once the bow is strung and bending evenly, it is very important that every time wood is removed it should be pulled by hand to about one-half draw fifteen or twenty times, taking care to never exceed full draw weight. This stresses the wood and reveals the true results of wood removal. Failure to stress the wood every time wood is removed results in "see-sawing": one limb is made weaker, then the other one made weaker, until the bow draws 30 pounds instead of the intended 45 pounds. It's primarily for this reason that kids love beginning bowyers.

> **WHAT I WISH I'D KNOWN**
> **Every time wood is removed the bow must be stressed while NEVER exceeding full draw weight. This stressing compresses the wood and reveals the true tiller of the limbs.**

When both limbs are bending smoothly and bending the same, as well as the thickness taper remaining perfectly even, it's time to weigh the bow.

In the old days, once a bow was drawing evenly, we'd pull it to full draw and note the weight. "Nope, too heavy, it pulls 74 pounds", and we'd remove more wood until the draw weight was what we wanted. Problem was, the bow was being stressed to 74 pounds, instead of the desired 45 pounds, so the limbs would take 74 pounds worth of set, or string follow, which robs speed. Occasionally, a marginal piece of wood would explode when drawn to a much higher weight than intended. That particular stave might have made a durable 45-pound bow, but couldn't withstand being drawn to the higher weight even once.

I knew a couple of commercial bowyers who would weigh a bow as soon as it drew evenly, note the weight, and immediately call it finished, whether 40 pounds or 75 pounds. That method worked after a fashion, but was highly inefficient if the goal was a bow of a particular weight.

There is a far better way to tiller. One that strains the wood by the least amount possible, and allows a bow to be precisely crafted to whatever weight is desired. (Tim Baker insists this method be called Jim Hamm Tillering, despite my objections, declaring it to be, "simply the most valuable tillering technique developed during the entire 10,000-plus years of archery history." This new approach came about as a direct result of discussions, aka arguments, between Tim and I while working on the first volume of *The Traditional Bowyer's Bibles*. I've agreed to include the designation here because of his insistence, not to mention that this is one of the few arguments I ever won with Tim.)

Using a measuring stick attached to a scale, draw the bow ONLY until it reaches the intended weight, and note the distance pulled.

This might be 45 pounds at 18 inches for a bow intended to be 45 pounds at 28 inches, telling us the bow is still quite a bit too strong, and rasping should continue evenly on both limbs to reduce weight. Or, the reading may be 45 pounds at 24 inches, which indicates the bow is getting close, and the coarse-toothed rasp should be replaced by a cabinet-maker's rasp with much finer teeth. Or a scraper can take the place of the rasp.

The draw-length reading at full draw weight indicates precisely how close the bow is to being finished and how much wood should be removed. Please read the preceding sentence again, as this is the key to tillering to the desired draw weight.

Don't forget to stress the bow every time wood is removed, no matter how small the amount, even just a few strokes with a scraper. The limbs must maintain a smooth, even bend, and both limbs must remain equal.

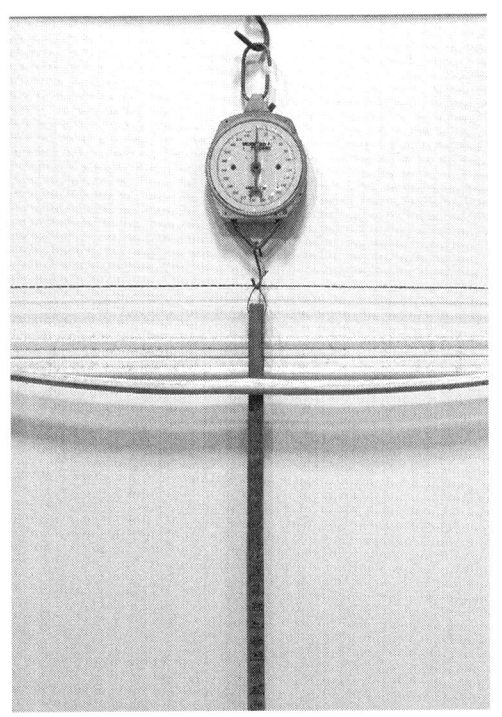

Scale setup for weighing a bow. Draw lengths are marked on the stick below the bow.

Bow is pulled only to final draw weight, and draw length noted.

> **WHAT I WISH I'D KNOWN**
> The draw-length reading at the intended final draw weight indicates how close the bow is to completion. As full draw length approaches, finer wood removal tools are more appropriate.

Continue pulling the bow to full weight until reaching 2 inches less than the desired draw length. At this point, unstring the bow and use a cabinet scraper or knife to remove any rasp marks or rough places. The "mountains" of the rasp marks contribute no strength

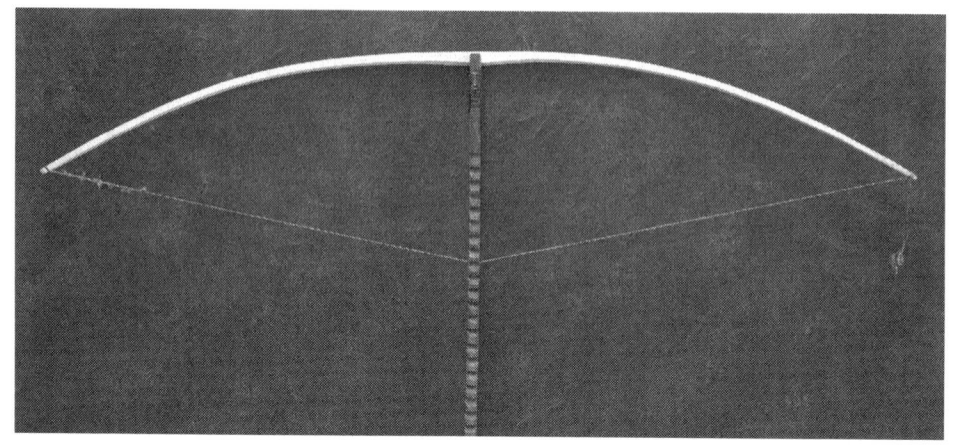

Correct tiller for longbow, half draw.

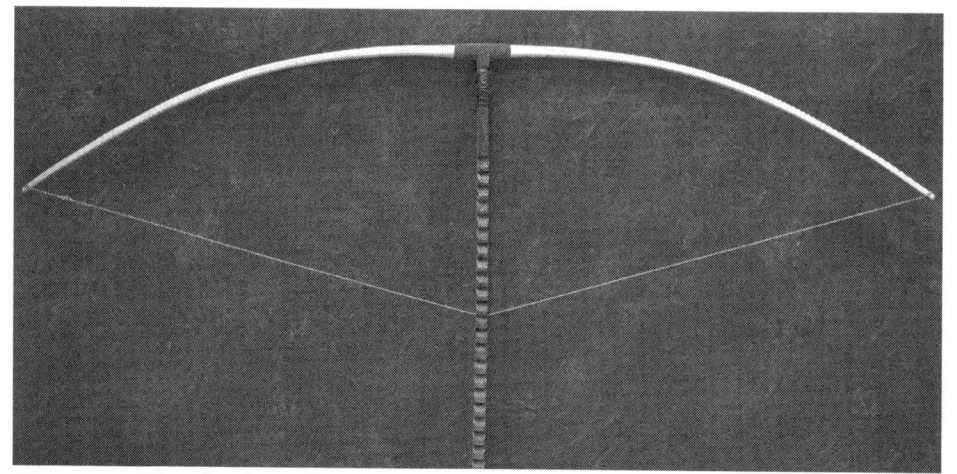

Correct tiller for longbow, full draw.

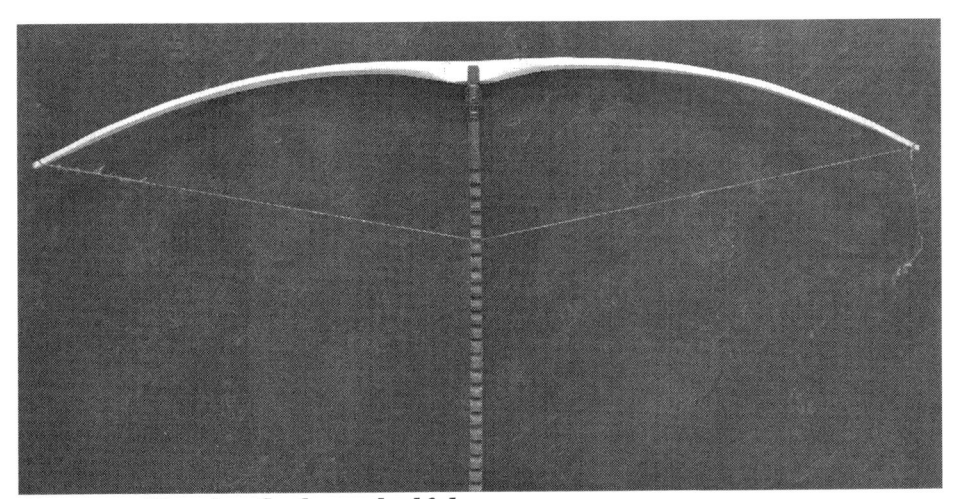

Correct tiller for flatbow, half draw.

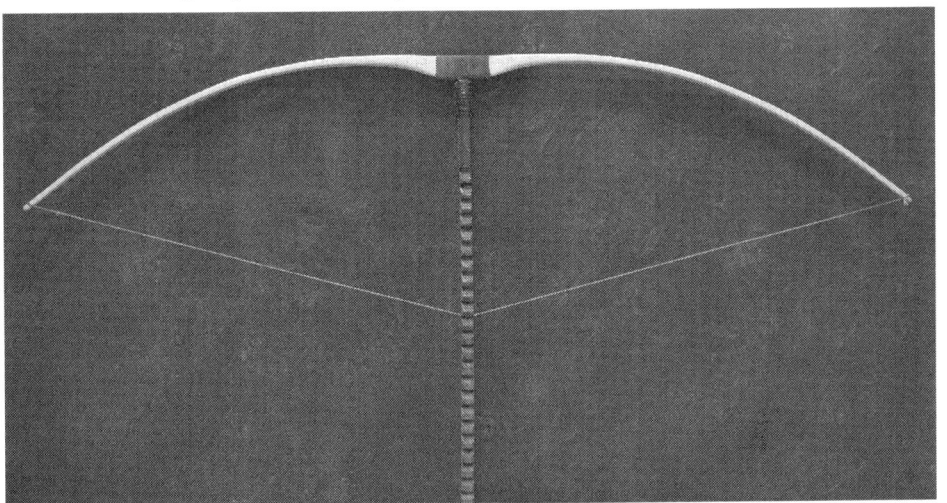

Correct tiller for flatbow, full draw.

to the bow, and thus can be removed without concern. However, scraping will remove some materials from all areas, reducing weight slightly, which is the reason to begin scraping at 2 inches less than full draw.

For scraping, hold the blade at right angles to the surface, it should scrape off thin shavings rather than cut. Round all the edges to about the diameter of a pea. Handle corners should be rounded even more, as the handle section is stiff enough not to bend at all. When using a scraper, whether a knife blade or cabinet scraper, if it starts to chatter (or leave washboards), immediately switch directions by 45° or even 90°.

When all rasp marks and imperfections are removed, weigh the bow again. At full draw weight, it should be about one inch short of full draw length. If more than an inch short of full draw length, sand the belly and sides only with 120 grit sandpaper on a sanding block. Weigh the bow often during this sanding until the bow is at draw weight one inch short of full draw length. Final sanding will take off just a touch more weight and land the bow right on target.

Don't hold a bow at full draw on the scale for more than a second or two. As the old bowyer's adage goes, "a bow at full draw is 9/10ths broken," and this is especially true when first pulling a new bow.

A couple of additional thoughts. First some tillering tricks. If a bow is drawing evenly, but is lighter than desired at full draw, cut an inch off of each limb and fashion new nocks. This will raise the weight by a couple of pounds. Or if a bow is at perfect draw weight, but one limb is slightly weaker, i.e. bending more than the other, then the weaker limb can be shortened by 1 ½ inches or so, and new nocks cut. The limbs should now be equal. These tricks are yet another reason why it's always a good idea to err on the side of making bows long, especially for beginners.

> **WHAT I WISH I'D KNOWN**
> **A moderate amount of string follow, 1 to 2 inches, indicates the bow was properly designed. It has as little mass as possible, while still having enough surface area to withstand the tension and compression forces.**

Regarding string follow, once a bow is pulled to full draw, the limbs will take a set, or follow the string to some degree. Minimizing string follow is desirable as it increases arrow speed. Assuming a straight stave or board with no inherent reflex or deflex, if a bow follows the string more than 2 inches, then either the wood wasn't dry enough, or the bow should have been designed longer and/or wider. Conversely, a bow can be overbuilt to a degree that it won't follow the string at all, but the increased mass will more than negate the slight arrow speed gains of the reduced string follow. Assuming a straight stave, a moderate amount of string follow, 1 to 2 inches, indicates the bow was properly designed. It has as little mass as possible while still having enough surface area to withstand the tension and compression forces.

Now that the bow is complete, once again:
Three Bedrook Rules of Bowmaking
1. Follow wood fibers on the back of the bow
2. Design bow for the specific gravity (density) of the wood species.
3. Tiller correctly.
Assuming sound wood, if a bow breaks, one of these rules was violated.

Finishing

The bow is now ready to heroically slay beasts. Or targets. But the final finishing steps will make it both more attractive and more durable.

The first step is sanding. Sand belly and sides with 220 and then 320 grit sandpaper, but not the back. Bows almost always break from the back, and taking more wood from the back will not make it stronger. Move on to 400 grit sandpaper, then sand the back, sides and belly. Continue with 600 grit. Don't worry if there are still small patches of the darker cambium layer on the back of the bow after sanding, they just add to the beauty and act as natural camouflage.

It's easy to think that sanding will take out any scratches or remaining rasp marks, but that's rarely the case. Sanding usually makes such imperfections more noticeable. When making the first pass with 220 grit, if such marks appear, it is better to gently scrape the area to remove them, then continue sanding.

Once the bow is sanded, it's advantageous to burnish the bow with a smooth bone or round tool handle. The best burnishing tool I've found is a small glass vessel such as a test tube. The flat portion polishes the flat areas, and the rounded end works into nooks and crannies of the bow, particularly on the back. It's best to burnish in the sunlight, where areas that have already been polished will easily reveal themselves. Apply moderate pressure, especially with the rounded end, because too much pressure will dent the wood. Go over the entire bow, paying special attention to the back.

This burnishing not only helps bring out the beauty of the wood, but compresses the surface and makes it more water resistant. In the case of the back and the belly, I believe it likely makes them slightly stronger and better able to resist the forces of tension and compression. In engineering terms, we are "work hardening" the surface of the wood.

After the sanding and burnishing are complete, some sort of sealer should be applied to help waterproof the wood. This sealer can be as simple as bacon grease or bear oil vigorously rubbed into the wood until friction warms the bow and oil, allowing the oil to permeate the wood fibers and cells. A fresh coat rubbed in before venturing afield in inclement weather works well, and I've made scores of bows with just such a finish.

Any type of penetrating commercial wood finish works fine, too, but surface finishes such as varnish can be too reflective and detract from the beauty of the wood. One of the best penetrating finishes is Formby's Tung Oil (not 100% tung oil, as it has drying agents which speed up the process). Applied with an old piece of cotton cloth, it soaks into the wood and fills the pores. Once dry, add another coat to further fill the pores and voids. After three or four such coats, the finish begins to build up on the surface, giving a lovely sheen that accentuates any colors or figure in the wood. Just make certain the latest coat of finish is completely dry before adding another.

An arrow rest is not an absolute necessity; after all, hundreds of generations of our ancestors shot arrows from the top of their bow hands with fine results. To do so requires careful attention to the smoothness of the feather attachments, as rough or sharp places here gaff the top of the bow hand as they pass.

Using an arrow rest allows better consistency from shot to shot, which is key to accuracy. The arrow rest can be carved from a wedge of wood or fashioned from several layers of harness leather, either of which can be attached to the bow with contact cement. Then a small piece of leather or fur can be glued to the top of the rest to damp the sound of the arrow when released.

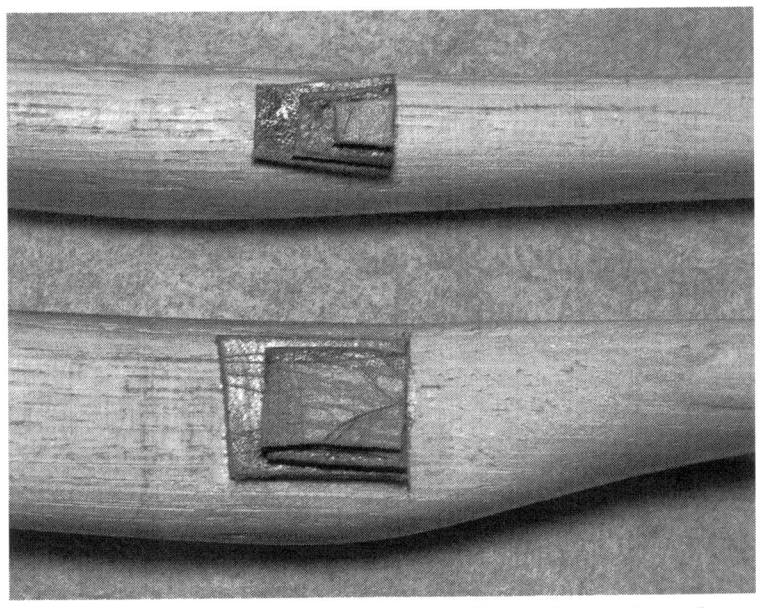

Harness leather arrow rest glued in place. Longbow, top; flatbow, bottom.

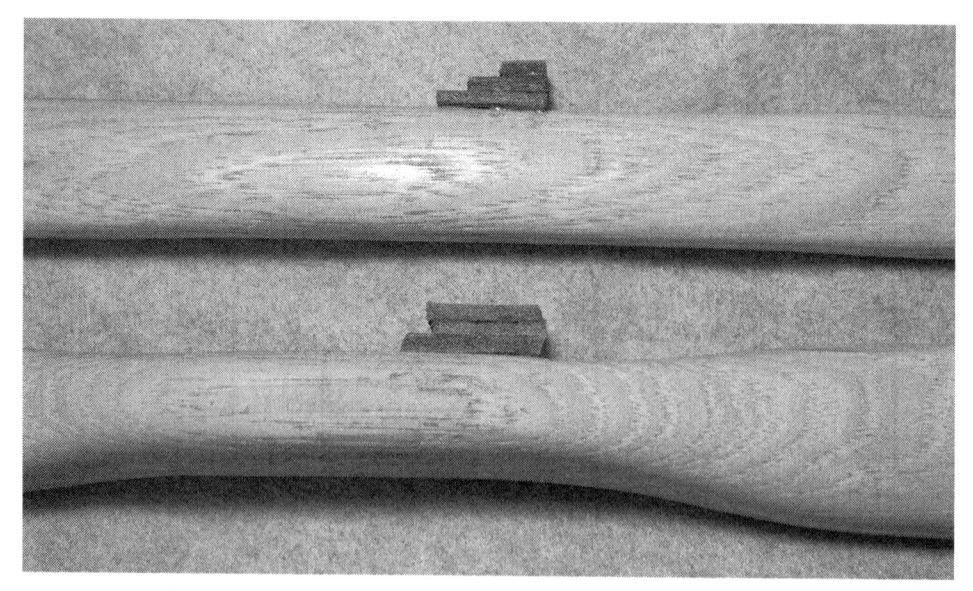

Note rounded edges of handle and limbs.

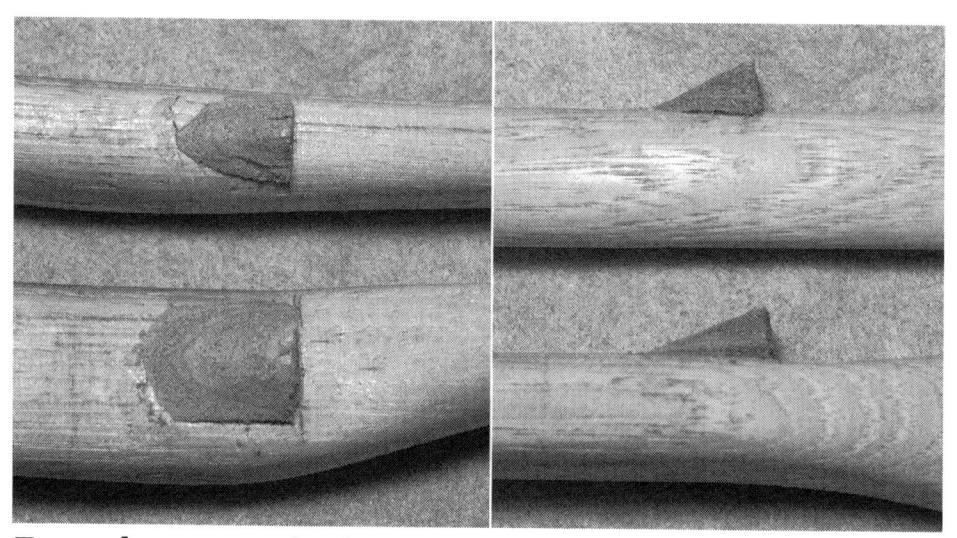

Tapered arrow rest leather. Longbow, top; flatbow, bottom

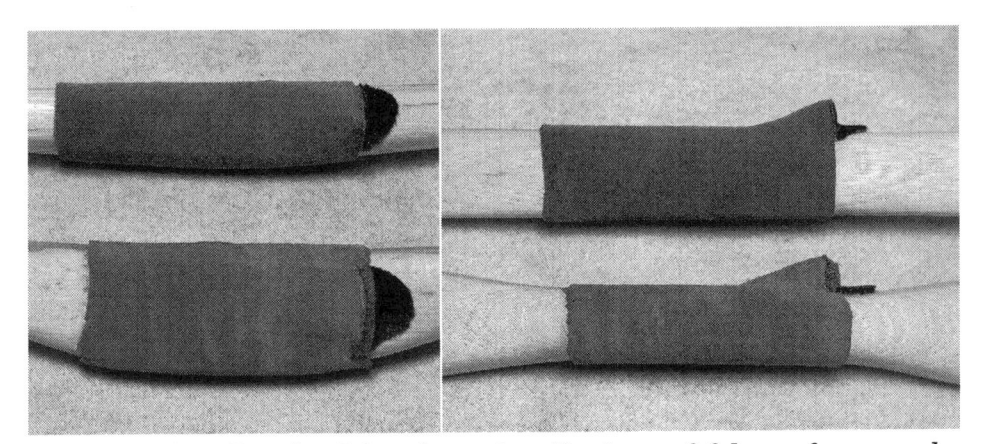

Buckskin handle glued in place. Small piece of felt or fur may be glued to arrow rest and bow to reduce noise when an arrow is released.

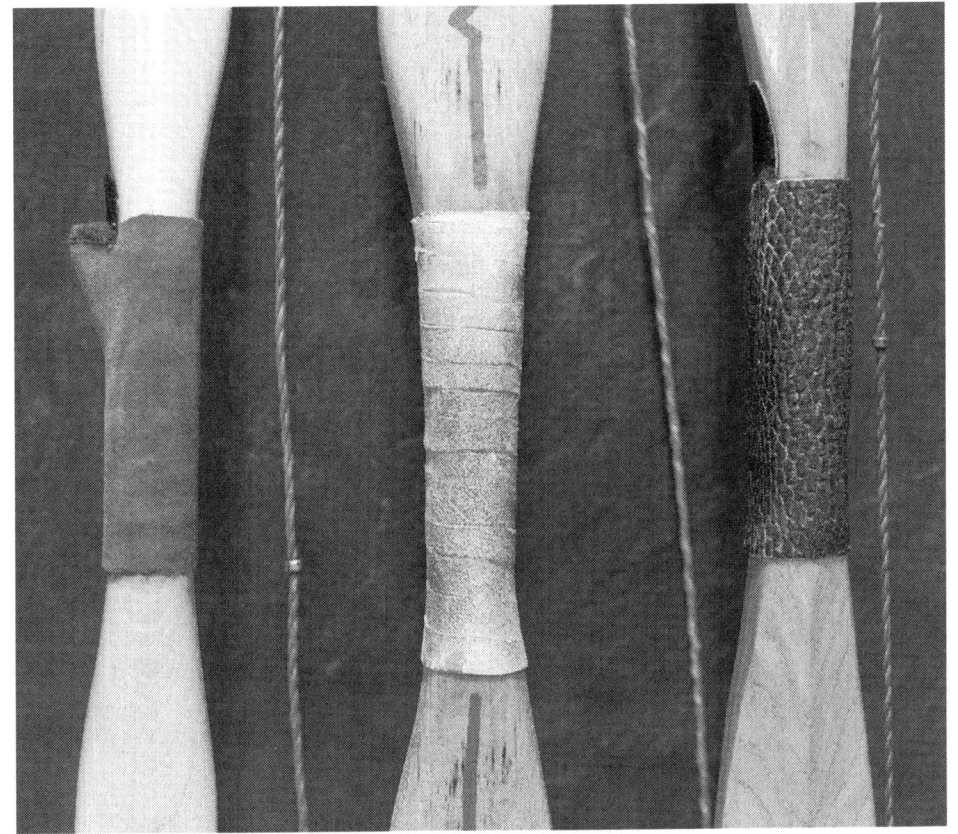

Covered handle examples. Left to right: glued buckskin, wrapped long buckskin thong, glued beaver tail skin. No covering at all is also an option.

With an arrow placed on the string of the strung bow and across the arrow rest, move the arrow nock until the arrow is exactly perpendicular to the bow. Make a mark on the string just above the arrow nock. Wrap a lump of thread or sinew around the string at this mark and secure it. This lump acts as a consistent arrow nocking point when shooting.

After the arrow rest is attached, and the nocking point placed on the string, the handle can be finished with a covering. Strips of leather wrapped around and around, a solid piece of buckskin glued into place, wrapped cordage (even including an extra bowstring), tennis racket handle wraps, flat sheets of cork and many more have been used for bow grips. Of course, thousands of bows throughout history have been perfectly serviceable with no handle covering of any kind.

The final step is signing and dating the bow, along with draw weight and draw length.

Indicate the draw weight and draw length, and also sign and date the bow.

One finishing refinement for hunters is string silencers. These silencers damp the twang of the string when an arrow is released, helping to prevent hair-triggered prey animals such as white-tailed deer from moving in that split second between arrow release and impact. Attach narrow strips of fur such as otter or beaver about 6 inches from each bow tip. Untwist the string and stick one end of the fur strip between the two bundles of bowstring threads, wrap the fur strip around and around the outside of the string, then stick the remaining end back through the center of the string to secure it. Pretty and effective.

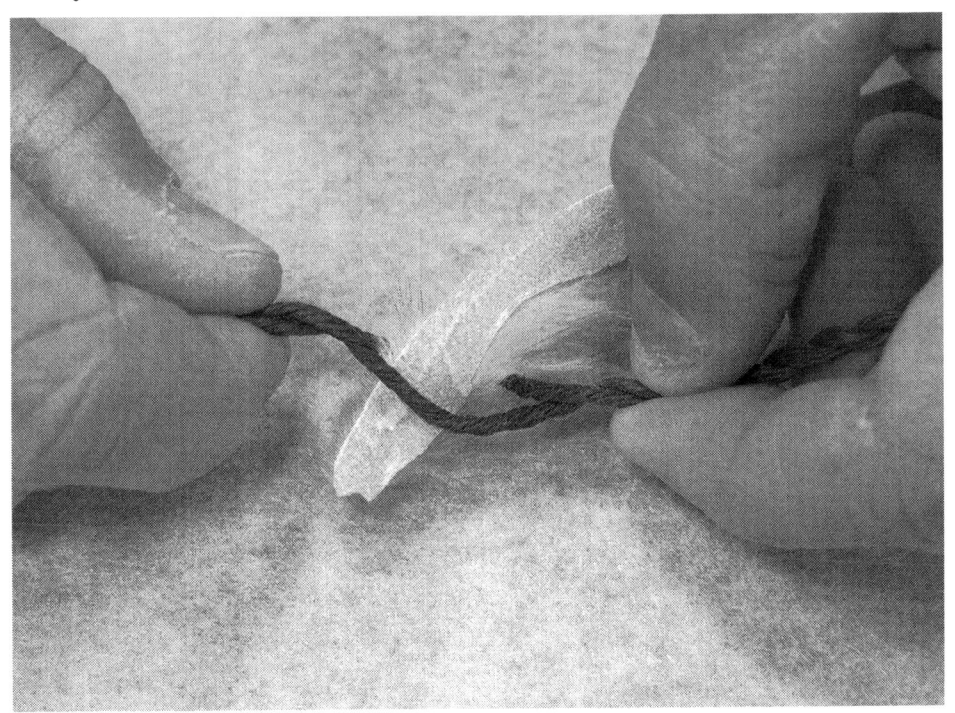

Place one end of the fur strip between the two string bundles.

Completed string silencer, one on each end of the string about 6 inches from the tips.

Arrows

Without delving into arrowmaking itself, here are a few thoughts on choosing wooden arrows for a new wood bow.

The shafts should be an inch or two longer than the archer's draw length. Some archers, myself included, when using commercial arrows, use full length shafts of 32 inches even if the true draw length is shorter. The extra length in front of the bow at full draw helps the sight picture as well as arrow flight.

Commercial wooden shafts are sorted according to the spine, or stiffness, of the shaft in five-pound increments; 40-45 pounds, 45-50 pounds, etc. The shaft's spine should be the same, or less, than the draw weight of the bow. For example, a 45-pound bow will use arrows spined for 40-45 pounds. When arrow flight problems occur, it's usually because the shaft is too stiff, which doesn't allow the shaft to bend around the handle and stabilize properly during flight, a phenomenon known as the "archer's paradox."

> **WHAT I WISH I'D KNOWN**
> When arrow flight problems occur, it's usually because the shaft is too stiff.

In general, slightly larger feathers fly straighter and exhibit better arrow flight than small feathers. They slow the arrow more rapidly due to the air resistance, but at ranges under 20 yards is scarcely noticeable. On commercial arrows, I specify 5 ½ inch shield-cut feathers. Such slightly larger feathers stabilize faster and are more effective when wet.

> **WHAT I WISH I'D KNOWN**
> Slightly larger feathers stabilize the arrow more quickly so it will exhibit better flight.

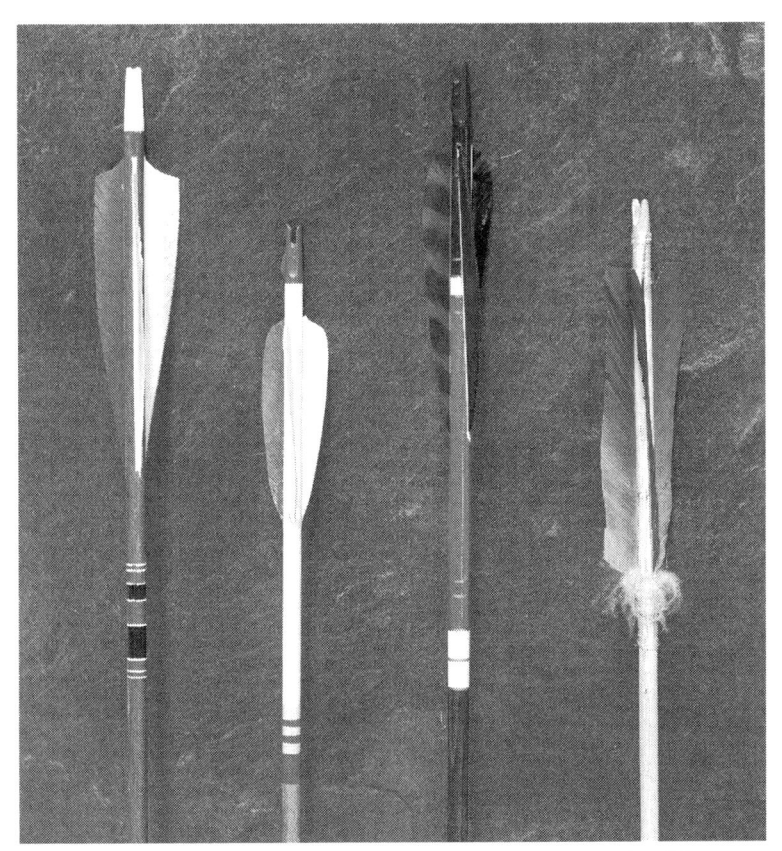

Different fletchings. Left to right: 5 ½ inch shield cut; 3 inch parabolic cut; 5 inch parabolic cut; straight taper. Note the feathers on the right are attached to the dogwood shaft with hide glue and sinew wrapping on each end.

    For hunters, a heavier arrow is desirable, at least 10 grains of arrow weight for each pound of bow weight, i.e., no less than a 500-grain arrow for a 50-pound bow. The heavier arrow penetrates better since it uses the bow's energy more efficiently. An added benefit of this efficiency is less energy left behind in the bow to make noise, thus the heavier arrows are quieter when released.

Shooting

The key to shooting well is consistent form, or performing the shot the same way every time.

Cant the top of the bow slightly to the right (for right-handers), so that when the bow is at full draw, the eye is directly over the arrow. This helps limit windage, or left to right variations.

The hand that draws the arrow is "anchored" to the face. A common anchoring practice is to place the tip of the middle finger at the corner of the mouth: the exact placement matters less than doing it exactly the same way every time.

Slightly canting the bow gives a clear sight picture and helps keep the arrow on the rest.

When at full draw, the archer should hesitate, "thousand one, thousand two," before releasing the arrow, preventing snap shooting or letting go of the arrow before reaching full draw. This is where a moderate weight bow really shines. It encourages good form, something impossible with a bow the archer struggles to bring to full draw. Never forget that accuracy and shot placement are far more important than arrow speed.

WHAT I WISH I'D KNOWN
Consistency is the key to accuracy. The steps to shooting consistently are:
- Anchor
- Pause at full draw
- Forearm of drawing hand parallel with the arrow
- Drawing hand flows straight back when the arrow is released
- Follow through; hold position until after the arrow strikes the target

At full draw, bow arm is straight; drawing forearm is parallel with the arrow.

Anchor point. One option is placing the tip of the middle finger at the corner of the mouth.

At full draw, the back muscles should create most of the force. Then, upon release, the drawing hand flows straight back, always in line with the arrow. Hold this position, or follow through, for two seconds after the arrow strikes the target.

> **WHAT I WISH I'D KNOWN**
> **Shoot at a blank bale for the first month. Concentrate on form by not using a target.**

When first shooting a traditional bow and trying to develop good form, shooting at a blank bale for the first month will be of great long-term benefit. Without an actual target, it's all about the form. Only after every aspect of the draw, anchor, release, and follow-through are natural and comfortable should a target be used.

You've Made Several Successful Bows, Now What?

Some make only one bow because they want to hunt with a weapon they've handcrafted. Others might simply wish to sample traditional archery and make a bow or two. There are folks who want to make a bow for their kids, nothing more. All of these are perfectly valid reasons to delve into wood bows.

For many, however, making wooden bows becomes an end in itself, even beyond hunting or target shooting. In our modern world, most everything is about efficiency and expedience, not so when dealing with wooden bows. Working with the wood is therapeutic; coaxing a bow from a stave takes as long as it takes with no time limits or pressure. As mentioned earlier, wooden bows are a time machine; not simply for the weapon produced, but also for the accompanying mindset.

So after making successful bows, the bowyer might well wish to start experimenting. Here are some thoughts on avenues that can be taken.

Make bows from woods requiring removal of sapwood to reach the dense heartwood: the bright yellow Osage orange, black locust, or black walnut. The bows won't necessarily perform better than those made earlier, but the color and beauty of the wood is electrifying.

Perhaps the bowyer is interested in a particular Native American tribe or the tribes from a particular area. Making such all-natural weapons entirely by hand is an ideal sought by many. With some research, native bows, arrows, and quivers can be precisely recreated, along with natural fiber strings and arrowheads.

Learn to deal with problems in wood, such as knots, cracks, or twists. In fact, many experienced bowyers gravitate to "character" wood, and seek out staves with challenging snaky grain or multiple knots, or make bows from small diameter trees or branches.

Try making bow tips narrower, which will increase arrow speed. The narrower the better, even to the extent of using pointed tips and unconventional nocks.

It's relatively easy to find suitable bow wood in 36-inch sections of trees, called billets, as opposed to 72-inch lengths. Splicing two billets together using a fishtail splice and gluing at the handle section yields full-length staves. Another related skill involving billets is making "take-down" bows. Using sockets or hinges at the handle section, the bows can come apart or fold in half, handy for storage as well as packing-in via canoe, pack horse, or floatplane.

Maybe the bowyer's interest leans more toward the shooting aspect. Seek out state or local longbow or traditional archery clubs, which often sponsor competitive shoots. Whether shooting 3-D animal targets set in the woods, or indoors using paper targets, the camaraderie and competition will quickly improve a shooter's skill.

The ultimate shooting challenge for many bowyers is taking game with their weapons. Just like the fly fisherman who ties his own flies, the hunter who takes game with his own hand-crafted bow counts two coups instead of one.

Though all of our distant ancestors made wooden bows, it's also a very singular path. Each individual chooses to fashion weapons and experiment for his own reasons.

Afterword

A young rural neighbor of mine, Jonathan Williams, recently asked for help making a wooden bow. He had been a compound hunter for several years, taking both whitetails and mule deer, but said he was looking for a further challenge, a way to take a step back from technology.

I explained to him the process described above. Over the course of several evenings, he dropped by after work, and we crafted his maple lumber bow. His finished D-bow was 74 inches long and drew 45 pounds at Jonathan's 28-inch draw length.

He shot it well from the first; his correct form allowing him to consistently place arrows in a 6-inch circle at fifteen yards. More than adequate for deer hunting purposes. I hoped the fact that he was already a bowhunter had inoculated him against the effects of surfing on the massive adrenalin flood that accompanies close-range encounters with a game animal.

He hunted hard on his ranch through the early season, willing to take any deer, doe or buck, with his handmade bow. In spite of near proximity on several occasions, he never so much as drew an arrow with predatory intent.

And then one Saturday morning, a cool front blew in. That evening, after dark, I got a call from him. He reported that he had shot at a buck with undetermined result, and wondered if I could bring my tracking dog over to take a look. By happenstance, my two grown sons, Lee and Reed, were visiting that weekend, so we loaded up my Blue Lacy dog, a breed well known in this area for being blood-trailers, and drove the three miles to Jonathan's house.

After meeting at his home, we followed him through several gates and stopped close to his ladder stand. He explained the setup. He had been surrounded by several deer, including a decent eight point. Finally, after waiting for the perfect opportunity, he managed to draw his bow at the buck undetected and released his arrow. He said the shot felt good but he didn't see or hear it hit.

So I whistled for my dog, which up to that time waited in the back of my pickup, whining with anticipation. He knew exactly why we were there and what his role would be. I hooked a long lead to his collar and showed him where Jonathan's buck had been. He circled a couple of times then took off like he was on rails, nose to the ground.

We all trotted to keep up, flashlights in hand.

After leading us through brush and cactus for a distance he stopped, took a hard right, and led us directly to the deer. Jonathan bolted forward, knelt down, and reverently touched the antlers. He had understated the buck, which was far beyond decent, a fine mature deer any hunter would be proud to harvest.

Handshakes followed all around, and during field dressing, my tracking dog got plenty of raw liver as his reward.

Jonathan's huge grin told the entire story. He had fashioned his own wooden bow, and with his first arrow in the heat of battle had proven himself a true predator. And by doing so, he joined an elite rank of weapons makers and hunters stretching back far beyond all written memory.

His forebears would be proud.

Appendix
WHAT I WISH I'D KNOWN

Three Bedrock Rules of Bowmaking:
1. Follow wood fibers on the back of the bow.
2. Design the bow for the specific gravity (density) of the wood species.
3. Tiller correctly.

If a bow breaks, one of these rules was violated.

Selecting and Cutting Wood

Beginners should start with whitewoods; ash, birch, cherry, elm, hickory, hop hornbeam, maple, and oak, among others.

Be very selective when choosing which trees to harvest.

Freshly cut whitewood can be taken all the way through the floor tillering stage, then quick-dried for 30 days, and the bow completed.

Rule 1: Follow Fibers on the Back of the Bow

Using whitewoods along with careful layout ensures the wood fibers are intact on the back of the bow.

Regarding lumber for bows: the growth ring lines on the flat side of the board, the bow's future back, are the edges of yearly growth rings, and must, MUST, be perfectly straight from one end of the board to the other.

Rule 2: Design for Specific Gravity of Wood

The primary wood quality a bowyer must know to properly design a bow is the specific gravity (density) of the wood species.

Different wood species impact bow design, but not bow performance.

When considering design, a longer bow is under less strain and easier to shoot accurately.

A moderate amount of string follow, 1 to 2 inches, indicates the bow is properly designed. It has as little mass as possible while still having enough surface area to withstand the tension and compression forces.

Strings
By using a timber hitch on one end, rather than two loops, the string is used as a tillering string first, then shortened to use for the bowstring.

Rule 3: Tiller Correctly
The thickness taper on the sides of the bow must always be even, with no thick or thin areas. If the thickness tapers are correct, then the bow will bend evenly.

Every time wood is removed, the bow must be stressed, while NEVER exceeding full draw weight. This stressing compresses the wood and reveals the true tiller of the limbs.

The draw-length reading at the intended final draw weight indicates how close the bow is to completion. As full draw length approaches, finer wood removal tools are more appropriate.

Arrows
When arrow flight problems occur, it's usually because the shaft was too stiff.

Larger feathers stabilize the arrow more quickly so it will exhibit better flight.

Shooting
A bow should be easy to shoot fifty times without tiring. An archer will find accuracy elusive if unable to reach consistent full draw.

   Consistency is the key to accuracy.
   Anchor
   Pause at full draw
   Forearm of drawing hand parallel with arrow

Drawing hand flows straight back when arrow released
Follow through, hold position until after arrow strikes target

Shoot at a blank bale for the first month. Concentrate on form, use no target.

Specific Gravity of Common Woods

Ash 0.55 to 0.60 depending on species
Birch 0.55 to 0.65 depending on species
Black Locust 0.69
Cherry 0.65
Elm 0.50 to 0.65 depending on species, cedar elm and winged elm are the densest
Hackberry 0.53
Hickory 0.65 to 0.72; pecan 0.66
Hop Hornbeam (Ironwood) 0.65
Maple 0.47 to 0.60
Mulberry 0.66
Oak 0.65 to 0.70 depending on species, though live oak is an exception at 0.85
Osage orange 0.80+
Walnut 0.55
Yew 0.65

Recommended Reading

Traditional Bowyer's Bibles
Collaborative book series by two dozen experts on every aspect of traditional archery. Their combined experience totals some five centuries.
All four volumes available from Amazon.

The Bent Stick
By Paul Comstock. This is Paul's groundbreaking first book. He's one of traditional archery's true pioneers, and one of only three authors who contributed to every volume of *The Traditional Bowyer's Bibles*.
Available from:
    The Bent Stick
    PO Box 1102
    Delaware, OH 43015
    $13.95 postpaid anywhere in the US.

Encyclopedia of Native American Bows, Arrows, and Quivers
Volume 1 – Northeast, Southeast, and Midwest
By Steve Allely and Jim Hamm

Encyclopedia of Native American Bows, Arrows, and Quivers
Volume 2 – Plains and Southwest
By Steve Allely and Jim Hamm
Required reading for recreating weapons from a particular tribe or region. Detailed full page 8 ½ by 11 inch pen and ink drawing of bows, arrows, and quivers from museums and private collections. Includes measurements, materials, and decoration.
Both volumes available from Amazon.

Bows & Arrows of the Native Americans
By Jim Hamm. Detailed instruction on making excellent arrows from scratch. Bowmaking info predates *The Traditional Bowyer's Bibles*. Available from Amazon.

Printed in Poland
by Amazon Fulfillment
Poland Sp. z o.o., Wrocław